How To Use This Book

Each page of this book is undated, so you can start writing anytime you want.
Each day, you only have to write only ONE good thing that happened at that day. If you want to write longer, there is a blank page at the end of every week.
That's it. Only one good thing a day.

Week 1

Some Thoughts...

WEEK 2

"Enjoy the little things, for one day, you'll look back and realize they were the big things." -Kurt Vonnegut

Sunday

Monday

Tuesday

Wednesday

Thursday

Friday

Saturday

Notes:

Some Thoughts...

WEEK 3

"everything has beauty, but not everyone sees it." ~ confucius

fri

sat

some notes

sun

mon

Tue

wed

Thu

Some Thoughts...

Week 4

"Gratitude turns what we have into enough." — Aesop

Sunday

Monday

Tuesday

Wednesday

Thursday

Friday

Saturday

Notes

Some Thoughts...

Week 5

"I still get wildly enthusiastic about little things... I play with leaves. I skip down the street and run against the wind." – Leo Buscaglia

Sun

Mon

Tue

Wed

Thu

Thoughts bubble

Sat

Fri

Some Thoughts...

Week 6

"The earth has music for those who listen."
~ george santayana

Sun

Mon

Tue

Wed

Thu

Fri

Sat

Notes

Some Thoughts...

Week 7

"The soul that gives thanks can find comfort in everything; the soul that complains can find comfort in nothing." – Hannah Whitall Smith

Notes:

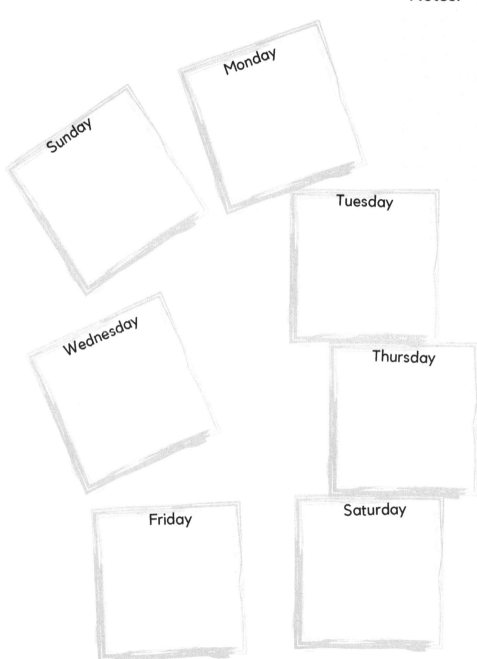

Sunday

Monday

Tuesday

Wednesday

Thursday

Friday

Saturday

Some Thoughts...

Week 8

"Gratitude helps you see what's there instead of what isn't"
- Unknown

Sunday

Monday

Thursday

Tuesday

Wednesday

Notes

Friday

Saturday

Some Thoughts...

Week 9

"Don't pray when it rains if you don't pray when the sun shines"
- Satchel Paige

tue

mon

sun

sat

fri

wed

thu

notes

Some Thoughts...

WEEK 10

"Gratitude is the greatest prayer. Thank you is the greatest mantra." ~ Swami Nithyananda

Sunday	My favorite part of the day	Monday
Tuesday	**Moment that I felt proud of myself**	**Wednesday**
Thursday	**Things that have been better than yesterday**	**Friday**
Saturday	**One thoughtful thing someone did to me**	**Notes**

Some Thoughts...

Week 11

"Never underestimate the significance of the little things done out of a large heart of love."
— Elizabeth George

Some Thoughts...

Week 12

"on earth there is no heaven, but there are pieces of it."
~ jules renard

Sun

Mon

Tue

Wed

Thu

Fri

Sat

Notes

Some Thoughts...

WEEK 13

"We often take for granted the very things that most deserve our gratitude." – Cynthia Ozick

Sunday

Monday

Tuesday

Wednesday

Thursday

friday

Notes:

Saturday

Some Thoughts...

Week 14

"One way to open your eyes is to ask yourself,
"What if I had never seen this before? What if I
knew I would never see it again?"
- Rachel Carson

Notes:

Monday

Sunday

Tuesday

Wednesday

Thursday

Friday

Saturday

Some Thoughts...

Week 15

"Gratitude makes sense of our past, brings peace for today, and creates a vision for tomorrow."
— Melody Beattie

Sunday

Monday

Tuesday

Wednesday

Thursday

Friday

Saturday

Notes

Some Thoughts...

WEEK 16

"you do not find the happy life. you make it."
- camilla eyring kimball

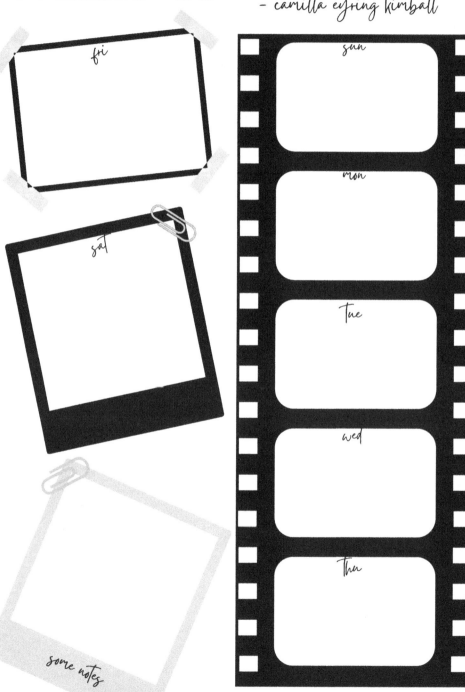

fri

sat

some notes

sun

mon

tue

wed

thu

Some Thoughts...

Week 17

"Be thankful for what you have; you'll end up having more. If you concentrate on what you don't have, you will never, ever have enough." – Oprah Winfrey

Sunday

Monday

Tuesday

Thursday

Wednesday

Friday

Notes

Saturday

Some Thoughts...

Week 18

"If I cannot do great things, I can do small things in a great way."
— Martin Luther King Jr.

tue

mon

sun

sat

fri

wed

thu

notes

Some Thoughts...

Week 19

"some people walk in the rain, others just get wet."
— roger miller

Sun

Mon

Tue

Wed

Thu

Fri

Sat

Notes

Some Thoughts...

Week 20

Some Thoughts...

WEEK 21

"It is not how much we have, but how much we enjoy, that makes happiness." - Charles Spurgeon

Some Thoughts...

Week 22

"The best and most beautiful things in the world cannot be seen or even touched - they must be felt with the heart." - Helen Keller

Sun

Mon

Tue

Wed

Thu

Thoughts bubble

Sat

Fri

Some Thoughts...

WEEK 23

*"don't take life too seriously.
you'll never get out of it alive."
- elbert hubbard*

fri

sat

some notes

sun

mon

tue

wed

thu

Some Thoughts...

WEEK 24

"No man is disturbed by things, but by his opinion about things."
- Epictetus

Sunday	Things I love about my body	Monday
Tuesday	My biggest accomplishment	Wednesday
Thursday	Things that make my life easier	Friday
Saturday	Talent /skills that I'm good at	Notes

Some Thoughts...

Week 25

"When the sun is shining I can do anything; no mountain is too high, no trouble too difficult to overcome." - Wilma Rudolph

Sun

Mon

Tue

Wed

Thu

Thoughts bubble

Sat

Fri

Some Thoughts...

Week 26

"nature does not hurry, yet everything is accomplished."
— Lao Tzu

Sun

Mon

Tue

Wed

Thu

Fri

Sat

Notes

Some Thoughts...

Week 27

"It's a funny thing about life, once you begin to take note of the things you are grateful for, you begin to lose sight of the things that you lack."
— Germany Kent

Notes:

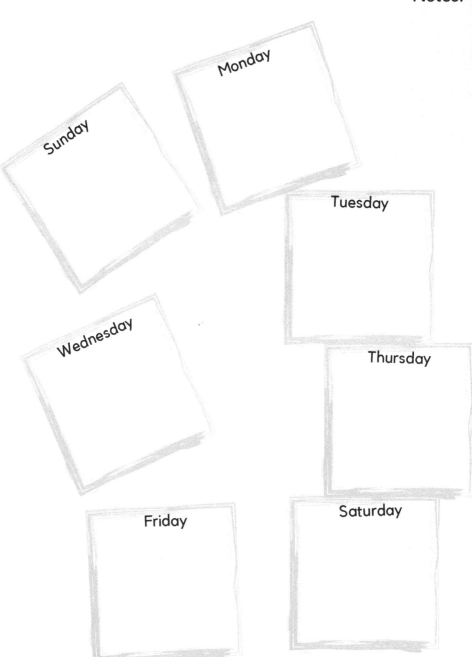

Sunday

Monday

Tuesday

Wednesday

Thursday

Friday

Saturday

Some Thoughts...

Week 28

"Focus on the good in each and every day, no matter what happens there is good to be found." -Catherine Pulsifer

Sunday

Monday

Thursday

Tuesday

Wednesday

Notes

Friday

Saturday

Some Thoughts...

Week 29

Some Thoughts...

WEEK 30

"A friend may be waiting behind a stranger's face."
-Maya Angelou

Sunday

Monday

Tuesday

Wednesday

Thursday

friday

Notes:

Saturday

Some Thoughts...

Week 31

"When you focus on the good, the good get better." -Unknown

Sunday

Monday

Tuesday

Wednesday

Thursday

Friday

Saturday

Notes

Some Thoughts...

WEEK 32

"you can only have bliss if you don't chase it."
– henepola gunaratana

fri

sat

some notes

sun

mon

tue

wed

thu

Some Thoughts...

Week 33

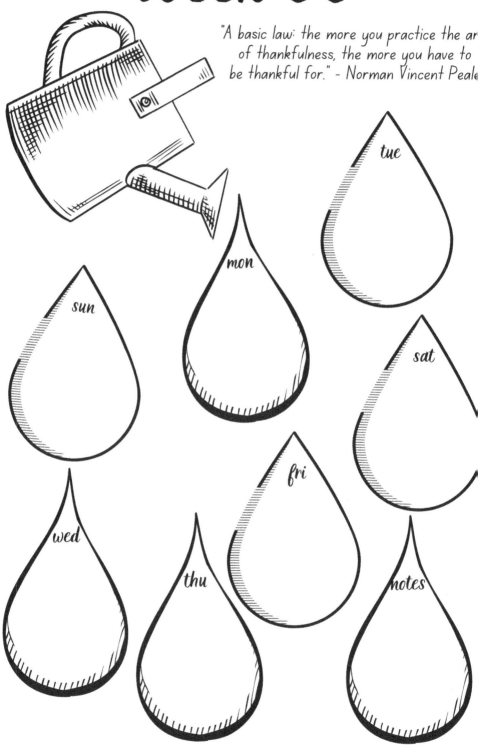

"A basic law: the more you practice the art of thankfulness, the more you have to be thankful for." - Norman Vincent Peale

sun
mon
tue
wed
thu
fri
sat
notes

Some Thoughts...

WEEK 34

"An attitude of gratitude brings great things."
- Harbhajan Singh Yogi

Sunday	Lucky things that happened to me	Monday
Tuesday	Someone I can't live without	Wednesday
Thursday	One thing I look forward everyday	Friday
Saturday	I laughed when..	Notes

Some Thoughts...

Week 35

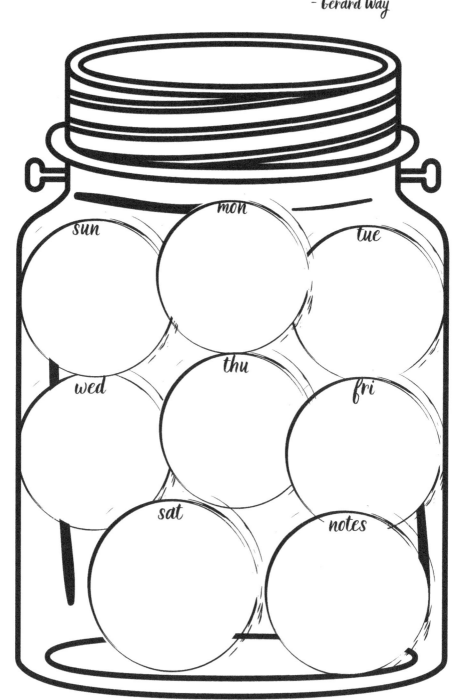

Some Thoughts...

Week 36

"There is a calmness to a life lived in gratitude, a quiet joy." - ralph h. blum

Sun

Mon

Tue

Wed

Thu

Fri

Sat

Notes

Some Thoughts...

Week 37

"Life is not just about the good things or not just about the bad things. It is both. It all depends where you focus your attention."
- Ann Marie Aguilar

Notes:

Monday

Sunday

Tuesday

Wednesday

Thursday

Friday

Saturday

Some Thoughts...

WEEK 38

"If you don't think every day is a good day, just try missing one."
-Cavett Robert

Sunday

Monday

Tuesday

Wednesday

Thursday

Friday

Notes:

Saturday

Some Thoughts...

Week 39

"Dwell on the beauty of life. Watc
the stars, and see yourself runnin
with them." - Marcus Aurelius

Sun

Mon

Tue

Wed

Thu

Thoughts bubble

Sat

Fri

Some Thoughts...

Week 40

"Learn to be thankful for what you already have, while you pursue all that you want." — Jim Rohn

Sunday

Monday

Tuesday

Wednesday

Thursday

Friday

Saturday

Notes

Some Thoughts...

Week 41

"There are better people in the world, do not let the worst do the worst to you, you deserve the best in life."
- Michael Bassey Johnson

Sunday

Monday

Tuesday

Thursday

Wednesday

Friday

Notes

Saturday

Some Thoughts...

Week 42

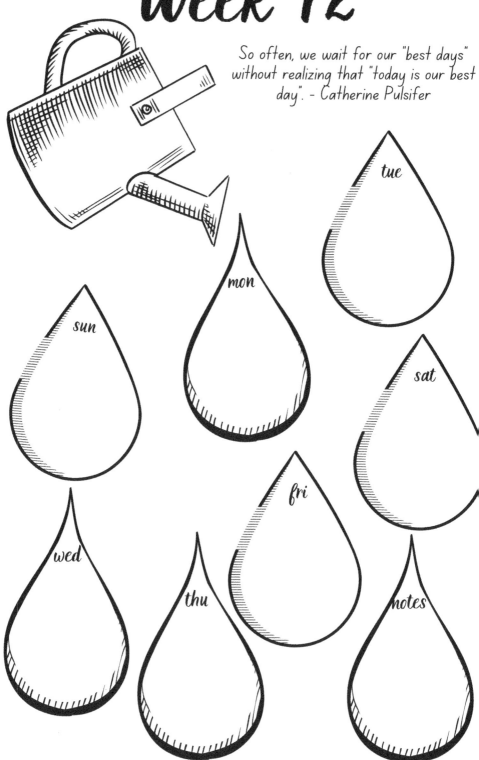

So often, we wait for our "best days" without realizing that "today is our best day". - Catherine Pulsifer

tue

mon

sun

sat

wed

thu

fri

notes

Some Thoughts...

Week 43

"wear gratitude like a cloak and it will feed every corner of your life." – rumi

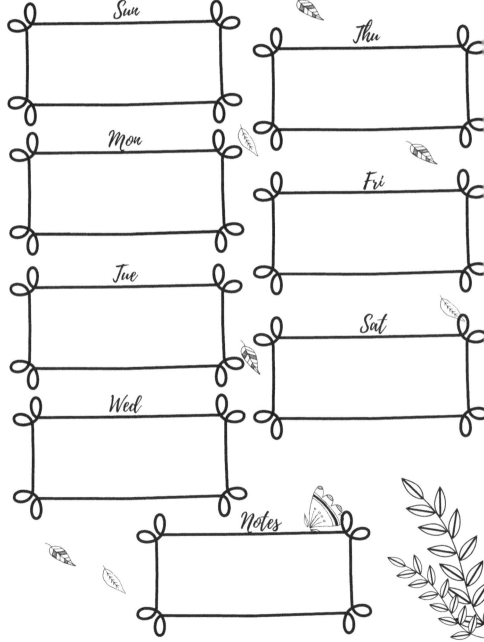

Sun

Mon

Tue

Wed

Thu

Fri

Sat

Notes

Some Thoughts...

Week 44

"There are always flowers for those who want to see them." -Henri Matisse

Some Thoughts...

WEEK 45

"If the only prayer you ever say in your entire life is thank you, it will be enough."
-Meister Eckhart

Sunday

Monday

Tuesday

Wednesday

Thursday

friday

Notes:

Saturday

Some Thoughts...

Week 46

"Happiness does not lead to gratitude. Gratitude leads to happiness." - David Steindl-Rast

Some Thoughts...

WEEK 47

fri

sat

some notes

sun

mon

tue

wed

thu

Some Thoughts...

WEEK 48

"When I started counting my blessings, my whole life turned around."
- Willie Nelson

Sunday	Moment I felt at peace	Monday
Tuesday	**Activity that makes me feel good**	**Wednesday**
Thursday	**Beautiful things I've seen**	**Friday**
Saturday	**My beautiful mistakes**	**Notes**

Some Thoughts...

Week 49

"Acknowledging the good that you already have in your life is the foundation for all abundance." - Eckhart Tolle

Some Thoughts...

Week 50

"A grateful heart is a magnet for miracles." - Unknown

Sunday

Monday

Tuesday

Wednesday

Thursday

Friday

Saturday

Notes

Some Thoughts...

Week 51

"Sometimes the little opportunities that fly at us each day can have the biggest impact." - Danny Wallace

Sunday

Monday

Thursday

Tuesday

Wednesday

Notes

Friday

Saturday

Some Thoughts...

Week 52

"To do a little good is more than to
accomplish great conquests."
- Buddha

Notes:

Sunday

Monday

Monday

Tuesday

Saturday

Wednesday

Sunday

Friday

Thursday

Some Thoughts...

Made in United States
Orlando, FL
19 December 2024

56189534R00059